THE
Archive Photographs
SERIES
OLD
SCOTSWOOD ROAD

Self-portrait of Jimmy Forsyth, a native of Barry in Wales, who came to work on Tyneside as a fitter in the 1940s and stayed to live in and portray the Scotswood Road area. From 1954 he walked round Newcastle showing people the local photographs he had taken and mounted in this album. The portrait was set up by a visiting photographer in 1981, the year Newcastle's Side Gallery exhibited Jimmy's work.

THE
Archive Photographs
SERIES

OLD SCOTSWOOD ROAD

Compiled by
A. Desmond Walton
with
West Newcastle Local Studies

CHALFORD

First published 1997
Copyright © A. Desmond Walton and West Newcastle Local Studies, 1997

The Chalford Publishing Company
St Mary's Mill, Chalford,
Stroud, Gloucestershire, GL6 8NX

ISBN 0 7524 0783 X

Typesetting and origination by
The Chalford Publishing Company
Printed in Great Britain by
Redwood Books, Trowbridge

Sheila Swinburne grew up at 536, Scotswood Road, where her father was a shop-owner. After winning a competition to become the Queen of the Blaydon Races centenary celebrations, she was taken on a series of photo-calls to publicise the event, in June 1962.

Contents

Acknowledgements

The compiler would particularly like to thank West Newcastle Local Studies colleagues, who like myself are volunteers and local pensioners, with a special mention of Fred Millican for transferring the accompanying text on to a word processor. Thanks go to Harry Bennett, Billie Cummings, John Hinds, Sheila O'Rourke, Terry Quinn and Ian Whillis. We meet together on Monday mornings to open up our Picture History Collection of many thousands of photographs and related material of west Newcastle stored at Benwell Library. When not dealing with enquiries we catalogue and process photographs while listening to Jimmy Forsyth reminiscing about 'Scotty Road' or looking through the contact prints we have done from his unique negatives. Derek Smith used the contact prints to compile his own *Scotswood Road* publication for Bloodaxe Books. We have done the same as part of a wider story.

Newcastle City Libraries and Arts allow us rent free accommodation and Benwell Library staff make us feel very much at home. Judy Forster, June Biggins and Maria Hoy have come from other libraries to give us support and to benefit from our local knowledge. Help has come from Gina Barron of Newcastle Discovery, Barbara Heathcote of Newcastle City Libraries and those who sit on local community committees to decide on the grants which keep us ticking over financially. Very many thanks. Local photographer Andrew Smith needs a special mention for unfailingly providing copy prints of a high standard.

Now the difficult bit! We would very much like to credit all those who have provided these photographs through donation, sale, or loan for copying. You will be giving a lot of pleasure to a wider audience than usual. Please accept our apologies for our failure to mention anyone. Some names we have recorded are; William Bell, David Clasper, Mrs E. Flint, Mrs S. Goldsmith, Cliff Heppell, Yvonne Gustard, Mrs P. Huggan, J. Longstaff, Newcastle City Libraries and Arts, Glynis Ovington, Jim Rawlinson, Sheila Shorrick (*née* Swinburne), Side Gallery, Alan Spires, Tom Steele, Mrs Thornton, Vickers Defence Systems (Peter McKenzie), Miss M. Wheeler, Steve Wood, Jean Youngs (*née* Raffle).

We appreciate permission to reproduce courtesy of the Chief Archivist, Tyne and Wear Archive Service for page 89 (both ref 1286/3), page 94 bottom (ref 161/484) and page 95 top (ref 161/489). Also courtesy of Prof. N. McCord, copyright University of Newcastle upon Tyne for page 68 bottom.

On 9 June 1962, Centenary Queen Sheila has just joined the procession from near Balmbra's in the Cloth Market. From outside the Cathedral here the route will lead along Collingwood Street.

Thomas Hair's painting of the Tyne Valley, *c.* 1860, shows the rural appearance of the area, as seen from Redheugh, Gateshead. In the top right corner between the fields of Elswick Hall and the riverside industry are the houses of Scotswood Road bounded on the south by the Newcastle to Carlisle Railway over viaducts. Near the island of King's Meadows can be seen the smoke from the factory of Armstrong's Works, behind the trees of Elswick Dene.

Introduction

Scotswood Road and the song *Blaydon Races*

The fame of Scotswood Road, Newcastle upon Tyne, today is mainly based on the fact that it is mentioned in the chorus of the song *Blaydon Races*. Although written in 1862 it has only been adopted as the Geordie anthem during this century. In various parts of the globe, when those who understand the Geordie accent come into contact, they can share a common heritage by singing a song about a journey by horse bus from Newcastle's Cloth Market to a race course on Blaydon Island on a Whit Monday, 1862. If they don't know the verses they can always belt out the chorus ending 'Gannin' alang the Scotswood Road to see the Blaydon Races'.

The popularity of the song stems from a book published before the First World War called *Tyneside Songs*. Local music hall singers revived the Geordie classics and *Blaydon Races* became a hit on newly introduced gramophone recordings. The chorus was taken up as a rallying cry by supporters of Newcastle United and soon their opponents began to learn the tune and identify it with the area. Soldiers in the First World War trenches sang it as a Geordie Tipperary to remind themselves of Collingwood Street, Armstrong's Scotswood Road factory and the Chain Suspension Bridge leading across to Blaydon.

Only the song remains today because the races at Blaydon are a distant memory after being closed down by the police after a disputed decision in 1916. Blaydon Island, which was the site of the race course in 1862, was removed from the Tyne from 1865. In 1887 the Races were revived at Stella Haugh. Geordie Ridley performed the song for the first time at the Harry Clasper Testimonial Concert organised by local business men and John Balmbra at the Wheatsheaf Inn, Cloth Market on 5 June 1862. Rower Harry Clasper is accepted as the finest sportsman locally in the nineteenth century. Today the Bigg Market, adjoining the Cloth Market, brings fame to Newcastle, as the focal point of the 'partying city' of Britain.

Scotswood Road's History

In the 1830s road and rail bridges were built across the Tyne at Scotswood and for the first time north-west Durham was joined to Newcastle through Benwell and Elswick. Scotswood Road gradually evolved as the road Newcastle citizens could take to the Chain Bridge at Scotswood, leading to Blaydon and Shotley Bridge.

In 1847 William Armstrong bought two west fields below Scotswood Road in the Elswick estate and opened a factory to build hydraulic cranes. After the Crimean War in the 1850s his newly invented field gun was accepted by the government for use by the armed forces. By the 1880s he was building warships at Elswick for several countries, including Japan. During the First World War the firm employed 57,000 men and 21,000 women at factories in Elswick, Scotswood and nearby. The population of Elswick between 1851 and 1901 had grown from 3,539 to 59,165. The Elswick section of Scotswood Road, one mile long, had a stretch of thriving shops and pubs opposite the factory. The whole area north from the Road to Westgate Road and beyond housing, churchess and shops. All were largely dependent on the economic health of Armstrong's.

Like other areas of heavy industry in the Depression between the wars widespread unemployment had catastrophic effects on a whole community. We have aimed to illustrate in this book some of the changes in the vicinity of the Road over more than a century. However, all is not gloom, there is a strength of the community spirit in adversity. Jimmy Forsyth's 1955 to 1965 photographs, taken during a period of disruption and demolition, do not show a cowed and depressed community. There is, instead, a liveliness, optimism and good humour which stemmed from the neighbourliness of the old streets when granny lived up the road and you could get anything you wanted on The Road.

Jimmy Forsyth

I first met Jimmy in the 1950s when I worked in Elswick library and I noticed him showing a great deal of interest in the history of the area. I was beginning to take more interest myself as I realised the imminence of widespread demolition and the disappearance of once familiar landmarks. What I didn't know was that Jimmy was a native of Barry in Wales and that he had lost an eye four days after coming to work on Tyneside at the end of the war. He then found work difficult to obtain, 'Nobody wants a one-eyed fitter', he said. He had the curiosity of a stranger visiting a foreign country and when he found that a building being pulled down near the town end of Scotswood Road was the old Infirmary mentioned in the *Blaydon Races*, he went to a pawn shop and bought a large box camera.

When I was based in an outer Newcastle library as West Area Librarian after 1974 Jimmy came to see me carrying a large album of photographs, contact prints from large black and white negatives. When I saw several more albums I realised he had been taking a record of the old Scotswood Road area, before, during and after demolition, followed by the construction of high rise flats. Because of my interest Jimmy asked me to keep his negatives in safe storage, 'Because if I die the lady who cleans out the flat will probably ditch them in the bin'. He has always been an independent loner but he likes mixing with people and even in his 80s is still out with his camera.

His negatives were used to mount a library exhibition and the enlargements from them proved very effective to illustrate the theme 'Scotswood Road with a Box Camera'. Derek Smith of the Side Gallery asked to borrow the negatives for exhibitions there in 1981 and 1986 and he then edited *Scotswood Road* published by Bloodaxe Books and did a documentary on Jimmy for Tyne Tees Television. In 1987 Jimmy won the Halina Award for Photography with the judges commending the pictures as having 'the photographic innocence and intuition which gives the pictures an all too rare sense of magic'.

Des Walton, January 1997, Newcastle upon Tyne

One

West From
Marlborough Crescent

The electric tram is approaching the beginning of Scotswood Road as it passes Marlborough Crescent bus station on the left. During 1996 buildings opposite the tram on both sides of the road were demolished to make way for Newcastle's millennium project, the International Centre for Life.

The first houses of Scotswood Road are on the left of this 1906 photograph. The sheep market behind the tram became later the Marlborough Crescent bus station. Work now goes ahead to make it the Millennium Project Bio Science Centre planned for completion March 1998. The building with the clock tower will remain. Architect John Dobson designed it as a cattle market office and toll house in 1831.

The original address of the King's Head (once called the 'Nut') was 1, Marlborough Street but it is now 2, Scotswood Road. On the right is Churchill Street. Note the street names associated with the Blenheim Palace family. There was a pub here in the 1830s, soon after the first houses were built. The present name is the courtyard.

10

The Newcastle Infirmary was built on the Forth banks facing the river outside the town walls, in 1751. Extensions designed by John Dobson were added in 1855. The 1862 Blaydon Races horse bus would pass near it when entering Scotswood Road and some travellers would return rather quickly after the wheel came off. If they didn't have a 'letter' for the Infirmary they might have to proceed to Dr Gibb, Westgate Road, or the dispensary in Nelson Street.

A view from Railway Street of the Infirmary buildings, c. 1950. Jimmy Forsyth purchased a box camera in 1954 to record the dismantling of the building. Excavations on the site for the Millennium Project Institute of Genetics foundations unearthed bodies from the infirmary cemetery.

The last remains of the old Infirmary buildings were being demolished in January 1994, when Jimmy took this photograph, forty years after he bought a camera to record the initial demolition. By 1994 he was very well known to workmen on these sites for he had obtained money for new films by selling them photos of themselves at work. This was preliminary work on the Millennium Project site.

On a Monday morning in 1967 there was usually a lot of activity at Newcastle's Cattle Market on the southern side of Scotswood Road. A car park was soon to take its place.

The west entrance of the cattle market in 1956 on the corner of Ord Street leading to the Redheugh Bridge. Note the beast's head on the arch. The Essoldo cinema advertising *The King and I* was in Westgate Road.

The Blenheim Hotel on the corner of Scotswood Road and Blenheim Street, 1966. The pub was demolished for the approach to a new Redheugh Bridge. Work is to start in 1997-98 on an inner-west bypass to replace Blenheim Street, on the left.

The 1930s darts team of Blenheim Street's Locomotive Inn.

By 1956 Blenheim Street had taken on a more multi-cultural aspect.

George Street next to Blenheim Street led north from the Road, with large terraced houses. In the 1920s the George I's manager George Steele, had organised a charabanc outing. The poverty in adjacent streets is exemplified by the youngsters on the left without shoes or stockings.

George Street led to Westmorland Road with the pub Villa Victoria, middle, near the junction. At least in Edwardian days there was plenty of room free from traffic for street children.

Back George Street lay behind the Farmers Inn, 98, Scotswood Road.

In 1935 these houses in Back George Street had stood for over a hundred years with very basic facilities. The Health Authority took a series of such photographs as a house clearance record and local youngsters were curious.

This is a 1930s view along Scotswood Road from near the Farmers Inn, with a butcher's boy ready to mount his bike. In the distance past the ends of Plummer Street and Hare Street was the site of the first pub on the south side of the Road, the Duke of Cumberland at No. 157.

The 1935 housing survey caption read 'back of Palace Street and elevated yard 105, Elswick East Terrace.' When seeing this view in a slide show an elderly lady identified the boy in front as her brother with the remark, 'He used to stand there all day as he was a cripple.' Houses were built round courtyards with shared toilets – and mangle!

In spite of the 1935 house clearance in Elswick East Terrace this was still typical of housing viewed from Scotswood Road in 1967.

The once affluent Rye Hill area was revealed when houses in the previous photograph were demolished in 1967. The flat roof of Cambridge Street School has the Charles Trevelyan building of Newcastle College behind it with St Mary the Virgin church nearby.

18

Hare Street leads off left to Railway Street and Redheugh bridge, 1956.

Jimmy Forsyth lived here in 1956, at No. 353, a downstairs flat, fourth door along from Falcon Motors. From here he sallied forth to take photographs of practically every street corner of the old Scotswood Road before demolition.

Jimmy now lives in the Cedars block of flats on the corner of Park Road and Scotswood Road. Jacky Longstaff visited him to take this photograph in 1987 after he received the Halina award for his work.

Living on Scotswood Road itself enabled Jimmy to be on hand when anything happened. He heard a screech of brakes outside and grabbed his camera with this result in 1958.

Business was thriving along the Road in 1910. Todd Bros was a popular store on the right (Nos 176/186) and did a lot of 'ticket' business based on tally men going round the streets to make weekly collections.

The Fountain, No. 126, was at the corner of Rye Hill, once a very affluent thoroughfare. In 1956 there was multiple occupation of large decaying houses and an interesting mix in the pub when actors vacated the Green room of the nearby People's Theatre.

Once a Presbyterian church this building was occupied by the People's Theatre in Rye Hill, near Scotswood Road, between 1929 and 1962. The photograph was taken by Steve Wood who presented his collection of prints and slides to Newcastle City Libraries and Arts in 1996.

Taken in the 1960s when sand blasting of old buildings transformed the appearance of Newcastle. This had once been a Baptist church in Rye Hill and later became the People's Hall Methodist Mission. Between 1954 and 1968 the adjoining manse on the left became the mission, before its closure. At the time David Allen, poster contractors, occupied the large old church.

Between Rye Hill and Maple Terrace, at the turn of the century this was Newcastle Royal Grammar School. From 1907 the building was taken over by Rutherford College Girls' School, until 1958, when the school transferred to the West Road.

Sarah Diamond and her family were very well known on the Road as shop owners. The usual garb for local men at the time was the regulation flat cap and muffler.

In 1956 the Diamond family owned the clothes shop on the right (No. 218). On the other corner of Ivy Street was the Royal Oak.

She was standing outside the Royal Oak, No. 222, when Jimmy was passing in 1956. From the poster you can see that Scotswood Road pubs had their own football teams.

The next stretch of shops to the west led to the Green Tree on the corner of Laurel Street, 1956.

After closing time at the Green Tree, No. 266, in 1960.

The corner window of the Green Tree consisted of a tree design in leaded panes. A green tree once stood here with seats around it for use when Newcastle people came for a country walk.

From Laurel Street to Gloucester Street (left) 1956. Gloucester Street's name derived from a house built on Westgate Road by a Newcastle shopkeeper whose business had been patronised by the Duke of Gloucester.

Gibson's fruit shop at the corner of Gloucester Street, 1956.

The Gibson family were in business in Scotswood Road over several generations. In this 1920s group outside Nos 284/6 Norah Gibson is second left. Her grandfather William was a Tyne oarsman in 1869 when James Renforth was the best man at his wedding.

Gibson fruit shop at 294, Scotswood Road on the corner with Gloucester Street, 1960.

Dicky Atkinson was always accompanied by his dog on the Road. Here he is in 1957. Gibson's doorway was a useful place for a rest after an evening stroll.

Behind this crash on the Road in 1960 can be seen Gibson's, right, Franks the barbers, the Co-op, a police box and Martin's bank. Soon all would disappear.

It is not surprising that road works were under way when Gloucester Street was part of the route Vickers-Armstrong used when testing tanks at the Ridsdale firing range, 1957.

By August, 1960, one side of Gloucester Street was being demolished. A chip shop and a Co-op are on the corner of Sycamore Street. Above the roofs can be seen the lead shot tower and gasometer which lay beind the Road.

If you crossed the Road from Gloucester Street you entered Dunn Street, now a main access road to the riverside. These workers could have come from the Marine Engine works, Gas works or Richardson's Leather Works below the railway bridge.

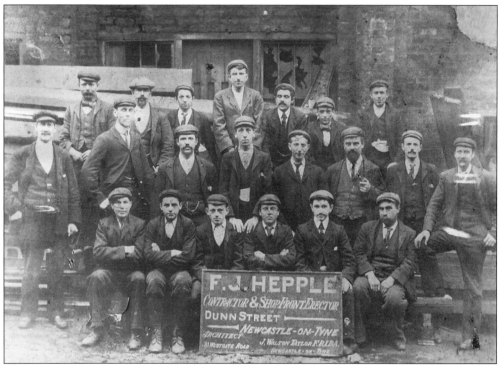

There were also many small firms in the Dunn Street area. Hepple's was at No. 40.

Most pubs were on Scotswood Road itself – as many as thirty at one time, although over fifty names can be quoted over a long period. The Skiff was well placed to catch riverside workers at 25, Dunn Street, on the corner of Railway Street. Far left is the Bath Hotel on the Scotswood Road corner.

Two

'Lads And Lasses, All Wi' Smilin' Faces'

The community spirit of the Scotswood Road area was based on neighbourly relationship within individual streets. Each street, however small, had its Peace Tea in 1919. It is ironic to think that these were followed by the hard days of the Depression, with only the Second World War to bring back employment.

Florrie Cullen, left, working in the London and Newcastle Tea Co., No. 346, on the corner of Suffolk Street, 1958.

Looking up Suffolk Street which led to Pine Street and Sycamore Street, 1958.

Peggy Moore had her hands full
looking after her shop and three
grand-children in 1959. The shop
stood at No. 185 near Hare Street.

Peggy knew how to keep the
youngest quiet for the photographer
in 1959. She stuck a Milky Way in
his mouth.

Knife grinder Charlie Francis stops outside a 'killing shop' near the cattle market to sharpen knives, 1958.

One of the few photographs recapturing the Teddy Boy fashions of 1957. These were tally men collecting in the Gloucester Street area for the ticket shops.

Dicky Atkinson with his dog and pals waiting for the pubs to open.

John Little in Penn Street getting ready for the Appleby fair, 1957.

Jimmy Wilkinson at Grey's coal yard in Railway Street, 1958.

A Cambridge Street resident in 1957. The old houses have gone but there is still a Cambridge Street, west of Newcastle College.

Jackie Prendergast and friend in Pine Street back lane, 1957.

Ann Prendergast with her hoola-hoop in 1957. She now lives in an outer Newcastle suburb. When Jimmy was complimented on the interesting light reflections on the wet road he replied, 'I wasn't looking for fancy shades.'

The Beveridge family of Gloucester Street took a personal interest in Jimmy. A granddaughter, Donna, still keeps an eye on him in 1997, in 1957 after he fell and broke an arm. Andrew Beveridge is on the pillion seat, here held by William.

Maureen, Stuart and Dorothy Beveridge on Easter Sunday, 1957.

Maureen Beveridge (left) and Lillian Winters in Pine Street, 1957. Behind Lillian is the corner of Charlotte Street.

A shy smile from Maureen Beveridge with a typical view of the crowded terraced housing behind the north side of the Road, 1958.

A change from the brick backgrounds of Jimmy's 1957 shots. Linda Gladders shows her feelings about being asked to put her arm round the neck of Robert Foster. Jimmy found that he could afford extra films by selling parents such photographs – but probably not this one!

Three generations in Cambridge Street back lane in 1960. Bob Wilson is seated.

Another three generations photograph, in the same back lane in 1960. Was the trap door on the left for coal or night soil?

Bethany Hall occupied a building previously owned by the Wesleyan Methodists and was listed in 1892 as Park Road church, Blenheim Street Circuit. It stood near Scotswood Road but attendances declined as people moved further north and Elswick Road church opened. Bethany Hall was demolished in 1961 and the church finally moved to Wingrove Road, Fenham, and closed in 1996.

Early in the twentieth century the houses in Park Road were desirable residences. The inter-war Depression caused a movement away by house owners but these two girls in 1959 exemplify resilience of the community through this period of decay and demolition.

This shop stood just west of Park Road at No. 412 and their relations still live in Fenham. There was a strong Jewish community living around the Road in 1916 and the Borsky firm of boot and clog makers and repairers were well patronised. M. Borsky is on the left and the other names in the group are Caro and Simbler.

Almost opposite the Borsky shop was the corner of Water Street where a shop had also once stood. On the site, entrepreneur Maurice Wilson had established a car salesroom in 1957.

On the other corner of Water Street, Maurice had established another salesroom for superior models. Sandy Skinner waits for customers in 1957.

Fire in Pine Street, 1959. The atmosphere of Jimmy's photographs has been compared with that captured by the artist L.S. Lowry in his painted industrial landscapes.

By 1960 the demolition teams were moving in. Jimmy probably sold a few prints to these Pine Street workmen.

Many of Jimmy's shots from 1960 were of buildings being demolished. This is in the Maple Street area.

Families still occupied adjoining houses during the demolition period. When they complained about the dust and mud workmen brought out sweeping brushes.

Three

From Park Road
To The Scotswood
Chain Bridge

The Clasper Arms was at the bottom of Park Road at Nos 404/8, Scotswood Road. The famous rower Harry Clasper lived on this site when it was 1, Armstrong Street in the 1860s. The song *Blaydon Races* was sung for the first time by its writer Geordie Ridley on 5 June 1862 for the Clasper Testimonial Concert at the Wheatsheaf Concert Room, Cloth Market, managed by John Balmbra. Local businessmen bought the house with the proceeds as Harry neared his retirement from rowing.

Contemporary advertisements for the Wheatsheaf Inn, Nos 3 and 4 Cloth Market, and for the Harry Clasper Testimonial in its concert room, 5 June 1862.

Below: Harry Clasper's boat races were often from Newcastle High Level Bridge to Scotswood Bridge, portrayed here. The *Blaydon Races* words are, 'We flew across the chain bridge right into Blaydon toon'.

The next street west of Park Road was Tulloch Street, with the Freemasons Arms on the corner adjoining St Stephen's church hall. Here it is in 1956.

Jimmy was back later with his camera when he saw a ladder against the hall in 1960. The result was this photograph of roof strippers.

Jimmy aged 47 in 1960 when the roof strippers took this photograph from the church hall roof. He still lives almost on this site today but the background is very different.

In October 1960, the sturdy church hall was almost down. Lord Armstrong and George Cruddas had helped to found it. It took a lot of knocking down.

A view across the Road in 1955 to the group of streets which were named after Armstrong's contemporaries in politics and engineering. He was a national figure after the Crimean War (1854-56) when his field gun was accepted by the government. Looking ahead up Hawes Street was De Grey Street – Lord De Grey was Minister for War at the time. To the west was named Brunel Terrace after Isambard Kingdom Brunel.

The Grapes Hotel on the corner of Hawes Street was demolished by 1960 but the Low Elswick post office and pillar box remained. A new view of St Stephen's Parish church emerged.

De Grey Street still stands here and so does St Michael's Roman Catholic church. In this view of 1961 the first flats of the Cruddas Park development are being built. The board reads Scotswood Redevelopment, a misnomer as Scotswood village is two miles west through Benwell. Historically the area is Low Elswick opposite the Elswick works. Herbert Street had stood in the middle of this site.

In June 1962 politicians Hugh Gaitskell and T. Dan Smith unveil the sculpture which aimed to typify the regeneration of the area. No one knows where this 'work of art' is now.

Leader of the Opposition, Hugh Gaitskell, was in Newcastle to attend the Blaydon Races centenary celebrations, 9 June 1962. To celebrate the centenary he opened the Willows flats. Behind him is T. Dan Smith whose ambition had been to make Newcastle 'the new Brasilia'.

Opposite the Gladstone Hotel at the corner of Clumber Street was the Rifle Hotel and part of Elswick Works, 1960. In 1854 the Duke of Newcastle was Minister for War and his residence was Clumber Park, Nottinghamshire.

Two boys between the Rifle Hotel rear and Elswick Works in 1960. A group can be discerned in the distance on Scotswood Road with the tower of St Stephen's church rearing up behind adjacent houses.

The flats of Haughton Court and King's Meadows, named after an offshore island once in the Tyne at Elswick, are nearing completion behind Clumber Street in 1960. In the left foreground a pile driver begins on the foundations of the Willows block.

In 1989 preparations for the Gateshead National Garden Festival were under way behind Dunston Staiths across the river. Vickers was now part of the new Scotswood Works but some Elswick Works buildings await demolition before a start can be made on the Newcastle Business Park. Today only the tower and spire of St Stephen's remain as a lasting landmark.

The street bordering Cruddas Park was named after Isambard Kingdom Brunel, whose son was an Armstrong's apprentice in 1863. The Cruddas family were Armstrong's directors and lived at Dene House, off the top left of this picture. They gave the park to the city. St Michael's Roman Catholic church, in the background in this 1958 photograph, is still functioning.

In the background, to the left, is Dene House, once the home of the Cruddas family and used during the 1990s by the Cyrenians. Nearby is Haughton Court flats named after the country home of the Cruddas, Haughton Castle near Humshaugh, Northumberland. The other flats are King's Meadows.

Opposite Cruddas Park the police station, fire station, baths and wash house stood, 1960.

Cruddas Park School was on the south-west corner of the park. The playground was on the roof, as too was the one at Cambridge Street School, a building which is now part of Newcastle College, Scotswood Road. The pub, the Dene, (No. 630) is to the left. Note the police box and drinking fountain in this 1956 photograph.

Sheila will later be riding in her coach in the opposite direction as the Centenary Queen. Here she takes a photo-call before an admiring customer of the Dene in 1962.

Newcastle tram No. 288, Class B, has come off the rails near Cruddas Park School. It is interesting to compare the headgear of the two groups of spectators.

A view from the north side of the Road of 27 and 28 Elswick Works shops in the 1960s.

A similar view showing No. 29 shop entrance in the 1950s.

The Mechanics Arms, No. 692, stood on the corner of Rendel Street, named after Armstrong's director George Rendel. The buildings alongside, opposite the works in 1956 still bore the inscription 'Elswick Factory School 1866' and 'Elswick Engine Works Mechanics Institute 1863'.

Staff of Elswick Factory School on an annual visit to Cragside for tea with Lady Armstrong in 1885.

The 1863 Institute, left, was a centre of adult education for many years. Before demolition it was used for various purposes including a staff library.

The original Crooked Billet lay close to the river, opposite King's Meadows island, before Armstrong's works were built in 1847. It moved to No. 734 at the bottom of Glue House Lane. It is reputed that at one time a glue factory stood here but one expert states that it was a 'blue' factory. Here it is in 1956.

In June 1962 the centenary procession has just passed the Crooked Billet and is now passing the notorious blocks of flats which had a short life in the Noble Street area.

Looking east past the Moulders Arms and Noble Street flats to the Forge Hammer (Nos 766/8) at the bottom of Edgeware Road, 1960.

The Gun Hotel at the bottom of Enfield Road, No. 818, 1956. It once had the famous boxer Seaman Tommy Watson as manager.

Part of the centenary celebrations was a veteran car rally. Here they are returning past the Crown cinema and the Gun Hotel in June 1962.

The centenary procession passes the Elswick Hotel left and Elswick Works right, viewed from the Hydraulic Crane.

The Hydraulic Crane was the last pub in 1996 from this section of the Road to be demolished, – two still stand at the town end. Customers wait for the procession to arrive.

Mrs E. Flint, manager's wife in the Hydraulic Crane (wearing glasses), helps out during the centenary celebrations.

Armstrong set up his factory in 1847 to build hydraulic cranes and it was situated just behind the pub site on the east boundary of Elswick estate. The window poster indicates the old pub nickname, the Old Toll Bar, because it adjoined the boundary with Benwell which was not part of Newcastle until the twentieth century.

The toll house and toll gate administered the 'Thorough Tax' for goods into Newcastle, c. 1900. Elswick Station to the right was situated in Benwell. This building was later used as a church mission.

A 1950s aerial view of the Elswick/Benwell boundary with the Hydraulic Crane pub, bottom right. The houses next to the cemetery, top right, parallel with Scotswood Road, were named after members of Richard Grainger's family. Streets to the left were named after the Buddle Atkinson family (Hugh, Frank, Clara and her husband, Revd Maughan).

The Scotswood Road end of the streets from Frank Street to Maughan Street, 1956.

A popular view down Clara Street across the road and river to the Dunston Power Station, 1955.

Looking east to School Street Co-op, past No. 1008, Ernie's the butcherss, 1956. As a boy one of Newcastle's best-known businessmen worked here for his father. He is now owner of Ken Bell International.

This charabanc stands at the bottom of Violet Street in 1922 outside Tommy Lee's shop. It would be a bumpy ride on the cobbles with solid tyres. The Depression was taking hold, notice the rather forlorn boy without shoes or stockings.

In 1862 the horse bus 'flew past Armstrong's factory reet up to the Robin Adair, just gannin' doon the railway bridge the bus wheel flew of there'. In 1962 this procession is approaching the point where the wheel came off.

When the wheel came off 'the lasses lost their crinolines and the veils that hid their faces, Aa got two black eyes and a broken nose gannin' to the Blaydon Races'.

On 25 March 1990, the Paradise Railway Bridge, known as the Skew Bridge, was demolished. Jimmy Forsyth was there to record the occasion and to snap fellow local historian, and present author, Des Walton. The bridge had been there since 1839.

Over the Tyne is Paradise village with its Methodist church and pitman's row. On the horizon, right, is St James' Benwell Parish church. Thirty-eight men and boys were drowned on 30 March 1925, when Scotswood miners broke through into the stagnant waters of the Paradise pit workings.

One of the last trains to cross the Paradise Bridge in 1956, viewed from the west.

Further west was the Boat House Inn, c. 1960. There had been an earlier pub on the site in the 1930s. Nearby was the entrance to the Delaval Drift mine, now marked by a plaque.

The Delaval Arms or the 'Trust' was unique in that it was erected in 1902 opposite the newly opened Scotswood works of Armstrong's by the Northumberland Public House Trust Co. Ltd as a 'practical scheme of Temperance reform'. Here it is around 1960.

Transport of a clearing press from the nearby Scotswood works of Vickers in the 1950s, with the Ord Arms and Jameson's Stores on the left.

A 'between the wars view' of a well stocked grocery store which was part of the Ord Arms building.

A view from near Scotswood Bridge of an early tram and the Ord Arms, 1906. The clock tower is now on top of the brewery buildings in Bath Lane.

Looking east at the procession, with a corner of the Ord Arms left, to Wheeler's dance hall adjoining part of Vickers, north of the Road.

Centenary Queen Sheila approaches Scotswood Bridge, 1962.

After being chosen as the Centenary Queen, Sheila took a photo-call and Vickers apprentices lined the bridge rails.

Toll house and toll gate of the Scotswood Bridge, one of the first four chain suspension bridges in the world.

When built in 1831 a report stated 'A situation more picturesque and striking ... could scarcely have been selected'. The architects were John and Benjamin Green, designers of the Theatre Royal. For the first time north-west Durham and Scotswood were brought into direct contact and Scotswood Road initiated.

Salmon fishers between the Scotswood railway and road bridges, *c.* 1914. Armstrong's workers complained about too much salmon in their diet.

The buildings on the other side of the bridge could be a shipyard which preceded Armstrong's Scotswood Works, *c.* 1890.

The new and old Scotswood Bridges in 1967.

Four

Scotswood Village And The 1925 Pit Disaster

A view from the road bridge of a regatta and Scotswood old village in 1926. Adamsez fireclay works are on the left and the village slopes up to Whitfield Road and the parish church in Armstrong Road. Part of Scotswood Road to Bell's Close is parallel with the river.

The trams stand in Bridge Crescent at the Scotswood Bridge terminus of Newcastle Corporation Tramways in 1938.

Trams 89 and 242, classes F and B at the terminus in 1939 with Adamsez offices and chimneys behind. The service also ran to Newburn and Throckley.

The Adamsez sanitary ware factory office on the left is still standing and is now occupied by a pie-making firm. Adamsez fireclay works closed in 1975. Off to the right is the section of Scotswood Road now under the western bypass Blaydon Bridge.

This display of sanitary ware was mounted on a float for the Blaydon Races centenary procession.

Ned Jose in 1950 when he worked for Adamsez as a fireclay miner in the seam underneath this part of Scotswood.

Adamsez used this aerial view to indicate various parts of the works in Scotswood around 1930. The railway bridge replaced earlier bridges dating from 1839 and has not been in use for some time. Denton Road is the well defined road stretching north and almost meeting Whitfield Road in the top corner. The Montagu pit lay off the top left corner.

Many street parties took place during May 1935, to celebrate the King George V Jubilee. This one was in Chapel Terrace with policeman 'Kirky' at the back. Two miners at the front are 'on their hunkers' as they would rest below ground.

The First World War memorial originally stood here, near the Co-op on Denton Road. It is now in the church grounds on Armstrong Road.

Denton Road descends past the end of both Lister Street and Fowberry Road and then past the Co-op, c. 1900. Just past the Co-op, poet Basil Bunting was born at No. 27, where his father also had his doctor's surgery.

From the worn appearance of the steps the houses must have been here for a century when the photograph was taken in 1934 for house clearance records. The steps (left) led up to No. 6 and next to the lady with baby was the rear yard of No. 5. Surely ripe for demolition!

Outside the Grace Darling on Denton Road with miners 'on their hunkers' in front, *c.* 1920. The building was later used as a surgery by Dr Harry Russell, a Newcastle Lord Mayor, whose wife, Theresa, was Newcastle's second lady Lord Mayor.

This print was presented by George Barclay, a miner who survived the 1925 Montagu Pit Disaster. Some of the 'Scotswood lads' were his marras in the 1920s.

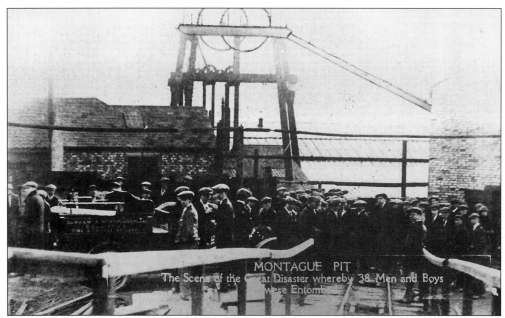

A postcard showing the pit head scene after the Montagu Colliery disaster on 30 March 1925. Miners from the View Pit or 'Low Monty' at the coal face had broken through into the old Paradise workings in Benwell. Thirty-eight men and boys were either drowned by the inrush of water or suffocated by black damp.

A group at the pit head after the disaster reading the local paper for news of their 'marras' trapped below.

Gathering near railway and pithead on Sunday 24 May 1925 for the first funeral procession to Elswick Cemetery. It illustrates a local saying, 'They were drowned in water and buried in water.'

On a drier day another procession winds along Scotswood Road on the way to Denton Road and Elswick Cemetery, 27 May 1925. Dickens Hypermarket was erected in 1996 on the site of the pit bank, top right.

A scene at Elswick Cemetery in June, 1926 after the grave stone and sculpture of a shepherd and miner was unveiled. In the background is the wall of the Jewish cemetery. Mine owners Montagu (without e) lived at Denton Hall, West Road, now next to the western bypass.

Five

Riverside Industry

A 1956 view from Redheugh Bridge of the Elswick Lead shot, tower demolished in 1969. A small community lived to the left of the picture until the 1950s round Mitford Street School. A power station may be erected there.

WALKERS, PARKER & Co. Ltd.

Lead Merchants and Manufacturers of

WHITE, RED, ORANGE, SHEET AND PIG LEAD, WHITE PAINT, LITHARGE, LEAD SHOT, PIPES, TRAPS, BENDS & SOLDERS.

BUYERS OF LEAD ORES AND SILVER LEAD BULLION.

ELSWICK LEAD WORKS, NEWCASTLE-ON-TYNE.

This advertisement was taken from the 1929 brochure of the North East Coast Exhibition.

West of the lead works and gasometers was Richardson's Leather Works and this is a view from across the river. On the left is Water Street, the eastern boundary of Armstrong's Elswick Works. The leather works was founded in Elswick in 1863 and was closed in 1970. Workers' families lived alongside the works in Water Street and Shumac Street and had the unique experience of being housed as a community, after 1970, in the Rye Hill area.

Children play next to the factory, c. 1910, while their parents sit near a greenhouse in a compact area between railway and river.

A scene which was typical of the friendliness of this small community, *c.* 1930. In the back lane between Water Street and Shumac Street (shumac was a bark for tanning leather).

The aristocrats of the tannery were the 'old time finishers' who chose their own working hours, *c.* 1900.

Working in the belt shop in 1898.

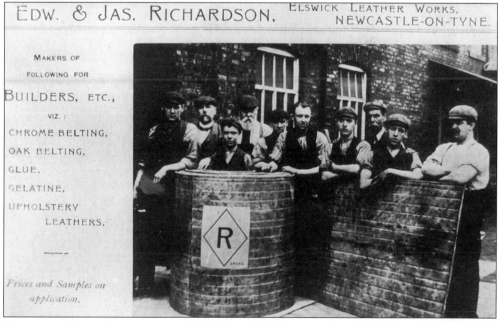

EDW. & JAS. RICHARDSON, ELSWICK LEATHER WORKS, NEWCASTLE-ON-TYNE.

MAKERS OF
FOLLOWING FOR

BUILDERS, ETC.,

VIZ. :

CHROME BELTING,

OAK BELTING,

GLUE,

GELATINE,

UPHOLSTERY
    LEATHERS.

Prices and Samples on
application.

Edward and James Richardson were Quakers and most members of the family lived in west Newcastle. One of their homes, originally called 'The Gables', was in Elswick Road, a building demolished in 1996. A family member was the shipbuilder John Wigham Richardson, and another was the actor, Sir Ralph Richardson.

W.G. Armstrong formed his engineering works in 1847 on the two fields, of the Elswick estate, an area of 7½ acres below Scotswood Road. Initially it produced hydraulic cranes and this is a drawing of the site in 1849.

Armstrong's was sufficiently important nationally in 1863 to attract premium apprentices from a wide area. H.M. Brunel, son of the famous engineer, is third from the left. He later played a significant part in designing Tower Bridge. Elswick Works built and installed a hydraulic pumping engine to operate the bridge bascules.

After the American Civil War, General Grant, centre, visited Elswick Works. Armstrong is on the right in the tall hat and in the background is a 100 ton gun.

Elswick shipyard opened in 1884 and the ship on the stocks is the *Panther*, a cruiser for the Austro-Hungarian navy. This view is from the island King's Meadows and the spire of St Stephen's church, is prominent, north of Scotswood Road.

The ill-fated battleship H.M.S. *Victoria* was built at Elswick in 1887 and is shown passing the Swing Bridge. The bridge was constructed in the engine works and installed in 1876.

A bird's-eye view of the works and housing to the north in 1887.

The blast furnaces constructed in the 1880s – later the site of 29 shop, Elswick.

The fire rescue squad based at the School Street depot.

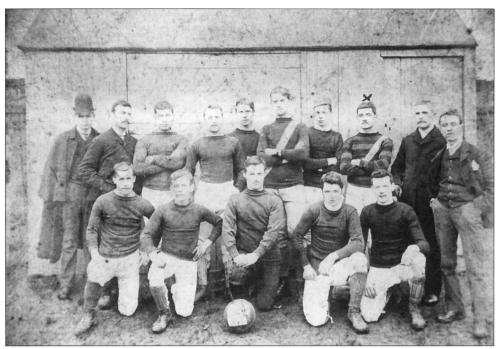

A football team including J.E. Heppell, a coppersmith, 1890s.

Men from Armstrong, Whitworth Ordnance Works who were members of the Elswick Battery during the Boer War, 1900. They were grouped on the veldt at Rooikraal, Transvaal. The photograph is from the scrapbook of Sir W.H. Stephenson of Throckley and Elswick.

Six twelve pounder field guns were made by Armstrong, Whitworth and presented to Lord Roberts during the Boer War. Some of the men who built the guns were formed into the Elswick Battery to man them. This was the most effective artillery unit in action.

A view of the shipyard in 1910. The last vessel to be launched here was the aircraft carrier H.M.S. *Eagle* in 1918.

Japanese Admiral Togo and party visited Elswick works in 1911 and were invited by Sir Andrew and Lady Noble to their home, Jesmond Dene House. Many Japanese Navy ships were built at Elswick.

Armstrong workers stream up Water Street after a night shift. The wall on the right marked the east boundary of the works and did not disappear completely until 1989 during clearance for the Newcastle Business Park.

The workers came up Water Street to catch trams standing on the Road. This view at the bottom of Park Road was taken on Saturday 12 February 1910 at midday, for a survey of overcrowding on trams in Newcastle.

A group of coppersmiths, including J.E. Heppell of Hampstead Road, in the 1900s.

Men have finished their shift and are crossing the Road to walk home or catch a tram, *c.* 1910. The bridge carried coal to the Tyne from North Elswick Pit which was behind Elswick Institute to the right of the photograph.

Sir W.G. Armstrong, Whitworth & Co. Ltd shipyard workers, *c.* 1910.

Pubs such as the Dene organised trips for off-duty workers. Foremen can still be distinguished by their bowler hats and silver watch chains, *c.* 1910.

This group were probably be waiting for the charabanc to arrive, at a time shortly before the outbreak of the First World War. It was a period of comparative affluence with a build up of orders for armaments.

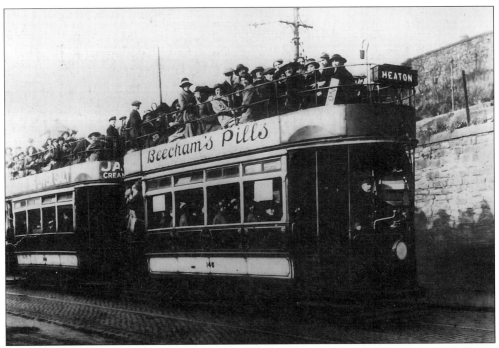

Trams collecting munition workers from Scotswood works, near Paradise Bridge in 1915. Trams were sometimes coupled up at this time.

The Elswick Battery during the First World War. They are moving up to go into action on the Somme, March 1918. The unit later became incorporated into the First Northumberland Volunteer Artillery as 203 (Elswick) Battery. An Elswick gun is now in the Territorial Army centre, Cowpen Road, Blyth.

A heavy gun machine shop in which 8 inch, 9 inch and 12 inch guns are being manufactured, *c.* 1916.

A 12 inch howitzer on a railway bogie attached to an ammunition wagon, *c.* 1916.

Munition workers off-duty with wounded soldiers during the First World War.

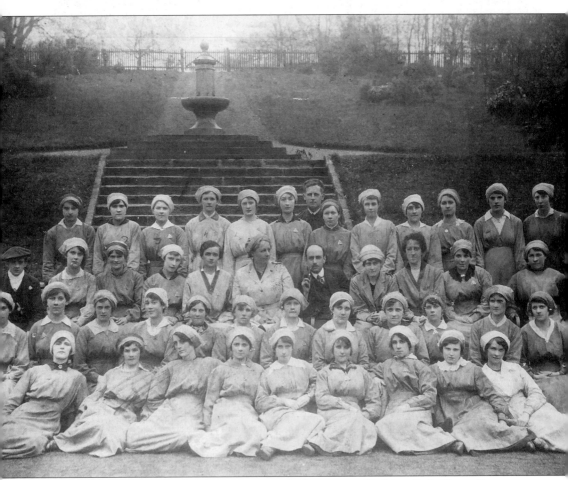

A group of munition workers posing next to the fountain in Hodgkin Park, Benwell.

Cartridge case stores were opened at several venues away from the main works – this one was at Derwenthaugh, *c.* 1916.

A locomotive being transferred to a barge for export to the East India Railways after Armstrong, Whitworth & Co. Ltd switched to peace time production in the 1920s.

Robert Smithson retired from his position as senior proof fitter at Armstrong in 1920, aged 79.

Robert's son Andrew and family, including Vera, both Armstrong employees, in the 1920s.

Senior proof fitter Andrew at Ridsdale Firing Range.

Andrew (white moustache) with a group at Ridsdale Firing Range, 1927.

Andrew's daughter Vera, extreme right, with other tracing office staff, etc. outside the Naval Yard Offices, 1970.

Vera, fourth from the right, retires from the tracing office in 1972.

Harry Spence presents Vera with a copy of Leslie Sansom's *Camera in the Works*, based on Vickers' photographs.

A group from 26 shop, Elswick Works in the 1930s.

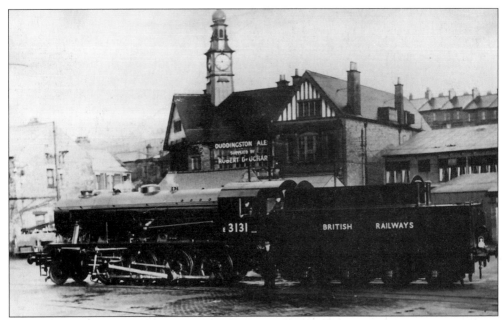

After the Second World War locomotives were reconditioned for British Railways. This scene is from 1946, with the Ord Arms and Wheeler's dance hall behind.

The chain bridge and Scotswood Works with a barge going up river to collect spoil from Stella Power Station, c. 1960.

Crankshaft 'shrinking' in 13 shop, Elswick in the 1950s.

Manufacture of valve assemblies in the 1920s.

The Shell Department organised this display for the King George V Jubilee, 1935.

T.W. Rowntree at work in the forge, 1949.

A group of 27 shop gaugers, E. Whittle, L. Bell and W. Noblett.

Excavations around a 100-ton jetty crane to check for safety of piles and foundations, *c.* 1950. The men are, from left to right: C. Parkin, H. Wodsworth, J. Fellows. The Scotswood chain bridge can be seen in the background.

Harry French, official photographer, takes a shot from the head office roof, *c.* 1950. Part of the headstock gear of Low Elswick Pit, at the bottom of Glue House Lane, is in the top right corner, near the Crooked Billet pub.

Apprentices with a model of a Clearing Press with all the parts laid out.

Scotswood Works retirement group with chain bridge behind. They had worked in the Maintenance Department.

N. Naylor, foreman, Water transport in the Traffic department, inspecting the loading of printing press rollers prior to transit to Scotswood Works. Dunston Power Station is in the background.

J. Crowe, W. Jeffrey, N. Pattinson and J. McGarry, foremen.

Mr A. Boddy, a fitter in 6A shop.

A steel foundry and pattern shop, Elswick team, winners of the Hitchin cup.

Queues in the library which was once the Mechanics' Institute opposite the works. Retired men came for a cash hand out at Christmas.

In the Delaval Canteen, Scotswood.

Six

The Geordie Anthem

The Centenary Queen waits outside No. 10, Cloth Market Cafe and Restaurant for the procession to start from Balmbra's, 9 June 1962.

Councillor Les Cuthbertson doffs his topper as the procession reaches the cattle market on the first stretch of Scotswood Road, called Marlborough Street, in 1862. The 1831 cattle market office, left, will be at the centre of the Newcastle Millennium Project, the International Centre for Life.

Part of the 1962 procession approaches the Hydraulic Crane pub with Elswick Works on the right.

Procession
spectators on a
patch of green,
used by workmen
to eat their bait,
between
Atkinson Road
and South View
Terrace houses,
top left.

The horse bus
approaches the
Scotswood
suspension bridge.
'We flew across
the chain bridge
reet into Blaydon
Toon'.

'The bellman he was callin' there – they called him Jacky Broon'. A few days before 9 June 1962, Sheila went to Blaydon to meet local Council Chairman J. Stephenson. They disputed whether Jacky's original bell belonged to Blaydon or Newcastle.

This 1847 plan of Newcastle Coal Districts shows the different venues for the Races. Between 1861 and 1865 they were on the island Dent's Meadows, usually called Blaydon Island. It is possible Geordie Ridley had attended the 1861 meeting and the 1862 song was based on this. His reference to rain in the last verse indicates that he added this verse later when a downpour at first stopped the horses wading across from Lemington. The final venue was Stella from 1887 to 1916.

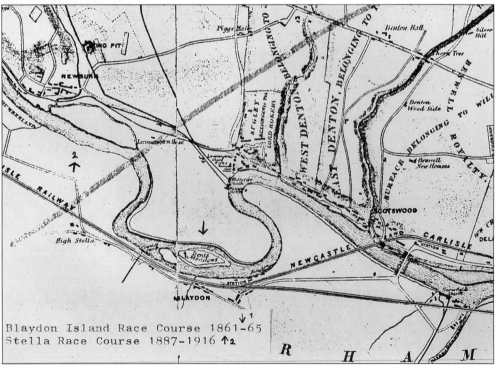

Blaydon Island Race Course 1861-65
Stella Race Course 1887-1916

BLAYDON RACES

Aa went to Blaydon Races, twas on the ninth of June
Eighteen hundred and sixty-two on a summer's efternoon
Aa tyuk the bus fra Balmbra's and she was heavy laden,
Away we went alang Collingwood Street that's on the road to Blaydon.

CHORUS:

> Oh! lads ye shud a' seen us gannin,
> Passin' the folks upon the road just as they were stannin.
> Thor wis lots o lads and lasses there all wi smilin faces
> Gannin alang the Scotswood Road to see the Blaydon Races.

We flew past Armstrong's factory an' up to the " Robin Adair ",
Just gannin' doon to the railway bridge the bus wheel flew off there;
The lasses lost thor crinolines an' the vails that hide thor faces;
Aa got two black eyes an' a broken nose in ga'n to Blaydon Races.

> Oh ! lads, *etc.*

When we gat the wheel put on, away we went agyen,
But them that had thor noses broke they cam' back-ower hyem;
Sum went to the Dispensary, an' sum to Dr. Gibb's,
An sum to the Informary to mend thor broken ribs.

> Oh ! lads, *etc.*

Noo when we gat to Paradise thor wes bonny gam begun,
Thor wes fower an' twenty on the bus, man hoo they danced an' sung,
They caaled on me to sing a song, aa sang them " Paddy Fagan ";
Aa danced a jig an' swung me twig that day aa went to Blaydon.

> Oh ! lads, *etc.*

We flew across the Chine bridge reet intiv Blaydon Toon,
The bellman he was callin' there—they called him Jacky Broon,
Aa saa him taakin' te sum cheps an' them he was persuadin'
Te gan an' see Geordy Ridley's show in the Mechanics' Haall at Blaydon.

> Oh ! lads, *etc.*

The rain it poored a' the day an' myed the groonds quite muddy,
" Coffy Johnny " had a white hat on—they yelled, " whe stole the cuddy?"
Thor wes spice stalls an munkey shows, an' aad wives sellin' ciders,
An' a chap wi' a ha'penny roondaboot shootin' " Noo me lads for riders ".

> Oh ! lads, *etc.*

Ridley first performed the song at the Harry Clasper Testimonial Concert on 5 June 1862, in the concert hall of the Wheatsheaf Hotel, Cloth Market. He was 27 when he wrote it and he died when 29. An accident at the age of 20 when driving a wagon led him to perform on the stage for a living. He gave himself a plug in the song as he knew that he would be performing in the Mechanics' Hall at Blaydon. All of his tunes were taken from other songs.

Many people think that this 1903 painting 'Blaydon Races' is linked with the song. Local artist William C. Irving may have based it on the popular 'Derby Day' to portray local low-life characters but none of the characters in the song are represented. In 1903 the race was held on Stella Haugh and this section of the painting shows the chimneys of Spencer's Steel Works, Newburn, in the background. The river and race course are in front of the steel works. The 1916 event ended in a dispute and closure by the police.